DISCOVER THE DIPLODOCUS

osh Gregory

**Our Prehistoric World:
Dinosaurs**

Published in the United States of America by:

Cherry Lake Press
2395 South Huron Parkway, Suite 200, Ann Arbor, Michigan 48104
www.cherrylakepress.com

Content Adviser: Gregory M. Erickson, PhD, Dinosaur Paleontologist, Department of Biological
Science, Florida State University, Tallahassee, Florida

Reading Adviser: Marla Conn, ReadAbility, Inc.

Photo and Illustration Credits: Cover: © Warpaint/Shutterstock.com; pages 4, 6: © Catmando/Shutterstock.com;
pages 7, 9: © Dariush M/Shutterstock.com; page 8: © Orla/Shutterstock.com; page 11: © Linda Bucklin/
Shutterstock.com; page 12: © David Herraez/Dreamstime.com; page 13: © Satori13/Dreamstime.com;
page 14: © PRISMA ARCHIVO/Alamy; page 15: © Daniel Eskridge/Dreamstime.com; page 16: © Elenarts/
Shutterstock.com; page 18: © metha1819/Shutterstock.com; page 21: © Presselect/Alamy

Cherry Lake Press is an imprint of Cherry Lake Publishing Group.

Library of Congress Cataloging-in-Publication Data has been filed and is available at catalog.loc.gov.

Cherry Lake Press would like to acknowledge the work of the Partnership for 21st Century Learning, a Network
of Battelle for Kids. Please visit http://www.battelleforkids.org/networks/p21 for more information.

Printed in the United States of America
Corporate Graphics

Note from publisher: Websites change regularly, and their future contents are outside of our control.
Supervise children when conducting any recommended online searches for extended learning opportunities.

CONTENTS

WHAT WAS DIPLODOCUS?

Diplodocus was a huge dinosaur. It had a long neck and an even longer tail. *Diplodocus* lived between 154 and 150 million years ago. Like all dinosaurs, it is now **extinct**.

Many scientists believe *Diplodocuses* lived in herds.

The name *Diplodocus* comes from Greek words meaning "double beam." *Diplodocus* was given this name because it had two rows of bones underneath its tail. These bones helped support the weight of the massive tail.

A *Diplodocus*'s tail was long and very heavy.

Think!

Why did *Diplodocus* need extra bones to support its tail? Have you seen any other animal with such a big tail? What would it feel like to carry such a big tail?

Diplodocus lived mainly in what is now western North America. This area was warmer long ago than it is today. It was also wetter. This weather helped many different kinds of plants grow. *Diplodocus* had plenty to eat!

The *Diplodocus* may have eaten water plants that grew around lakes and swamps.

WHAT DID *DIPLODOCUS* LOOK LIKE?

Have you ever seen a giraffe at the zoo? Imagine if its tail were even longer than its neck. It would look a lot like *Diplodocus*! *Diplodocus* was one of the largest dinosaurs. A fully grown *Diplodocus* was usually about 85 feet (26 meters) long. Some could grow even longer! These huge dinosaurs weighed around 18 tons. That is about as heavy as six cars!

Diplodocus's tail could be almost twice as long as its neck.

Diplodocus had a huge body. But its head was very small. It also had a very small brain. This means it was not a very smart dinosaur.

Diplodocus's **skull** had a long shape. It had long front teeth and no back teeth.

Diplodocus had a very small brain for an animal its size.

Crest

13

Diplodocus had large feet with five toes, just like modern elephants.

Create!

Try making a model of *Diplodocus* out of clay. Be sure to shape its long neck and tail. Give it big legs to keep it from falling over!

Diplodocus had wide legs to support its huge body. It had long back legs and shorter front legs. Its shoulders were closer to the ground than its back end was. Each leg ended in a wide foot. Each foot had five toes.

Diplodocus stood on its back legs to rear up high. Today, scientists believe it could not bend its neck up. Its muscles were not built like that.

HOW DID DIPLODOCUS LIVE?

Diplodocus was an **herbivore**. It used its front teeth to bite leaves from plants. *Diplodocus* did not have any back teeth. It probably swallowed its food without chewing. Scientists are not sure which plants it ate. It may have reached into the treetops for leaves. It may also have eaten plants that grew on the ground.

Diplodocus could use its heavy body and big feet to scare or hurt an enemy.

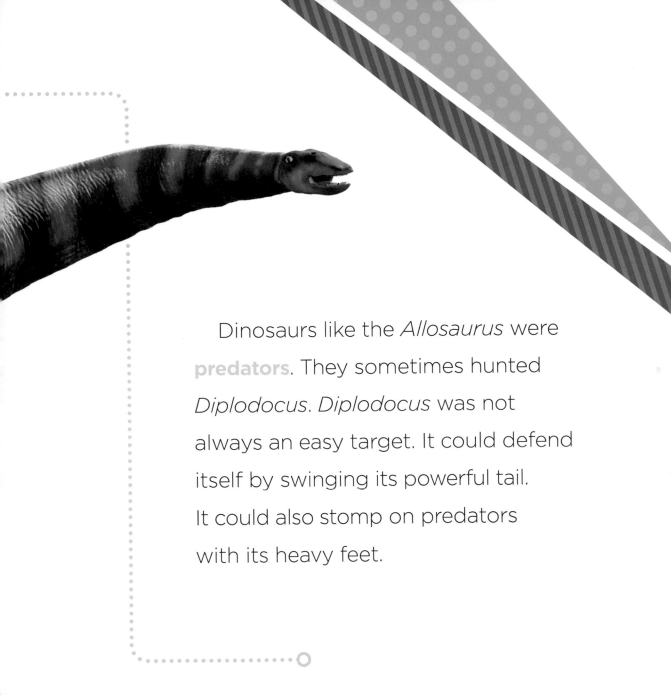

Dinosaurs like the *Allosaurus* were **predators**. They sometimes hunted *Diplodocus*. *Diplodocus* was not always an easy target. It could defend itself by swinging its powerful tail. It could also stomp on predators with its heavy feet.

Scientists study dinosaurs and other extinct animals by looking at **fossils**. A scientist named Samuel Williston found the first *Diplodocus* fossils in 1877. Over a hundred skeletons have been found since. These fossils have taught us a lot! *Diplodocus* skulls are much harder to find. There are only a few that have been recovered.

Make a Guess!

Why is it so unusual to find *Diplodocus* skulls? Think about where fossils are found. Think about what you know about *Diplodocus*. What might have happened to the skulls? A teacher or librarian can help you find the answer.